IMAGES
of America
PORT COSTA

In an 1848 expedition through the Bay Area, William Heath Davis (1822–1909) reported seeing vast herds of elk crossing the strait near present-day Port Costa. This drawing by E. Wyttenback from Davis's book *Seventy-five Years in California* illustrates Davis's description. The Davis story is one of the proposed explanations for the name "Bull Valley," wherein Port Costa now sits.

ON THE COVER: In this c. 1915 photograph, friends and family gather near the ferry terminal to watch a train depart for Martinez. Lynch's California Hotel and the Ferry Exchange Hotel are visible in the background.

IMAGES
of America
PORT COSTA

John V. Robinson and Veronica Crane

Copyright © 2007 by John V. Robinson and Veronica Crane
ISBN 978-1-5316-2830-7

Published by Arcadia Publishing
Charleston SC, Chicago IL, Portsmouth NH, San Francisco CA

Library of Congress Catalog Card Number: 2006924392

For all general information contact Arcadia Publishing at:
Telephone 843-853-2070
Fax 843-853-0044
E-mail sales@arcadiapublishing.com
For customer service and orders:
Toll-Free 1-888-313-2665

Visit us on the Internet at www.arcadiapublishing.com

Contents

Acknowledgments	6
Introduction	7
1. The Age of the Ferryboats	9
2. The Railroad Years	29
3. Bull Valley	37
4. The Port Costa Brick Works	83
5. Eckley	111

Acknowledgments

Many people had a hand in the creation of this book. Betty Maffei and the staff at the Contra Costa Historical Society were gracious, as always, in allowing access to their collection. Likewise, Keith Olsen and Leo Cid at the Crockett Historical Museum were invaluable resources.

From Port Costa, Bill and Betty Ligon, Jim Thomas, Don and Mary Ann Robinson, and Theresa Jurik all made valuable contributions. Mary Ann McLendon and her brother Chuck Mossina made an especially valuable contribution to the portion of the book devoted to the Port Costa Brick Works. Their father, Lawrence Mossina, worked at the Port Costa Brick Works for 50 years. During his years of employment, the elder Mossina took hundreds of photographs of every aspect of the plant's operations. The collection of photographs is an invaluable record of the company's history. That Lawrence Mossina took so many photographs over so long a period of time is testament to his devotion to the Brick Works. The fact that Chuck Mossina had the presence of mind to keep the photographs is nothing short of miraculous. The view of the Port Costa Brick Works presented in these pages is a mere fraction of the material in the Mossina collection. Another local, Lewis Stewart, is known to have photographed the town extensively since his arrival in the early 1970s. Lewis has graciously allowed use of several photographs in the present book. This book would not be possible without the help of such generous people.

INTRODUCTION

Port Costa sits in a little valley that was once part of a 4,000-acre ranch owned by William Piper. The original ranch house and barn are thought to be still standing; the Port Costa Mercantile building is believed to be the remodeled old barn. Port Costa, as it is known today, came into existence in 1878 when the Central Pacific Railroad started to build its southern ferry transfer slip at the mouth of what was then called Bull Valley. No one is sure why the site was called Bull Valley. Two stories are told to explain the name. Some people think it came from the herds of bull elk that William Heath Davis reported seeing crossing the Carquinez Strait in 1848. Another popular tale asserts that Mexican cowboys used bulls to drive the Native Americans out of the valley.

Since the site was the ferry's Contra Costa County port, the terminal was dubbed Port Costa. The first ferry, *Solano* (named for the Solano County terminal in Benicia), went into service in December 1879 to provide a faster method of getting trains from Solano County to Contra Costa County. The narrow channel and deep water made the Carquinez Strait an ideal location for the train-transfer ferry. At the time, the *Solano* was the largest ferry in the world. With the arrival of the railroad and ferry terminal, development was swift along the south shore of the Carquinez Strait from Martinez to Crockett.

The railroad attracted businessmen like George W. McNear who, in 1880, built Port Costa Warehouses and Dock Company west of the ferry terminal. McNear was an ambitious man and, in July 1883, McNear bought William Piper's ranch for $100,000 and started to lay out the town of Port Costa that we know today. Under McNear's stewardship, Port Costa prospered and was once the busiest port on the West Coast, shipping Port Costa grain around the world.

For 50 years or so, the bulk of Port Costa's business activities were on wharves built along the shoreline. Aside from the wharves and warehouses, the waterfront consisted mainly of hotels, saloons, and general stores that catered to the hundreds of railroad men, stevedores, and sailors who worked the waterfront for about $3 a day, paid in gold.

Port Costa's success attracted a diverse population. Old newspaper accounts and informal oral histories tell of villages adjacent to Port Costa, including the Mexican Village and a place called China Camp, east of Port Costa, for the Chinese laborers working for the railroad. The exact location of these villages or their dates of existence is unknown, and no trace of them remains. To the author's knowledge, there are no photographs that document the Mexican and Chinese contributions to Port Costa's early development. Any additions to this aspect of Port Costa's history would be most welcome.

Over the years, the waterfront suffered a series of catastrophic fires: 1883, 1889, 1909, 1924, and 1941. The docks were rebuilt in 1883 and 1889; in the subsequent fires, the docks and warehouses were not rebuilt. As the grain market declined and shipping interests moved to San Francisco, the waterfront portion of Port Costa slipped into decline. Waterfront Port Costa survived the many fires and the 1906 earthquake before finally succumbing to the toredo pile worms. The old waterfront town was demolished in 1921.

In 1914, a second ferry, the *Contra Costa*, was put into service to handle the increasing demand to transport trains across the strait. All told, Port Costa hosted two of the largest ferries in the world for 50 years. The ferryboat era ended in 1930 when Southern Pacific Railroad opened a railroad bridge across the Suisun Bay between Benicia and Martinez, and east of Port Costa. When the two great ferryboats were retired from service, Port Costa's rowdy waterfront era passed into history.

For the next 30 years, Southern Pacific maintained a railroad yard at Port Costa. The railroad activity kept the Bull Valley portion of Port Costa vibrant. In 1960, the Southern Pacific Railroad moved its operations to Martinez, and Port Costa slipped into dormancy for a few years.

The modern era began in 1963 when Arkansas native Bill Rich discovered the dormant community and, like G. W. McNear a century earlier, saw a good business opportunity. Rich bought several buildings in the business district, including McNear's three-story concrete warehouse (built in 1886), the Burlington Hotel (built c. 1883), and McNear's two-story office building (built in 1897). Rich set to work renovating the structures and in a few years had reinvented the town as a tourist attraction with restaurants, a refurbished hotel, and dozens of antique shops. That incarnation of the town withered in 1983 when a fire devastated the hills between Crockett and Port Costa. Eckley was obliterated, and several homes in Port Costa were also destroyed. The aftermath of the fire seemed to diminish the tourist trade, and many of the antique shops closed.

Today, with its rollicking years in the past, Port Costa is slipping back into dormancy. The warehouse and Bull Valley Restaurant still attract people, and the Burlington Hotel is still open, making Port Costa an attractive tourist destination. The winding roads leading into town meander along pastures and park land before dropping down into the quiet Bull Valley and dead-ending at the waterfront, where the railroad's roundhouse once stood. Hikers along the trails of the Carquinez Regional Shoreline Park can see the remains of the old pilings of old waterfront Port Costa. Since most buildings in Port Costa are more than 100 years old, visitors today come to experience a piece of Contra Costa County's rich history.

One

THE AGE OF THE FERRYBOATS

Ferryboats *Solano* (left), constructed in 1879, and *Contra Costa* (right), constructed in 1914, are docked in the Port Costa slips c. 1920. Both ferries were over 400 feet long—the largest in the world at that time. For 50 years, the ferry service between Benicia and Port Costa was a vital link in the transcontinental train service. (Courtesy of Contra Costa Historical Society.)

Above is a detail from a c. 1928 aerial photograph showing the town near the end of the ferry service. On the left, Port Costa docks are still in use. The crater-like depression, known as "the volcano" by locals, is visible at the bottom left of the frame. Waterfront Port Costa is gone, and the two ferry slips are seen with the *Contra Costa* in one of them. Below is a northerly view of the massive California Wharf and Warehouse Company, which sat between Eckley and Port Costa until fire claimed it in 1924.

Pictured above, in another detail from the same aerial photograph, the storage tanks of Associated Oil are visible on the hillside above the Port Costa Brick Works. The Associated Oil docks have replaced the Black Diamond coal-storage facility, and the Port Costa Brick Works can be seen to the right. The photograph below shows the Black Diamond coal-storage facility and the western mouth of the Nevada Docks in the background as they looked around 1900. The old waterfront suffered fires in 1883, 1889, 1909, 1924, and 1941. Warehouses and businesses were quickly rebuilt after the early fires. After 1909, docks and businesses destroyed by fire were not so readily rebuilt.

Seen above is the Port Costa waterfront looking east. The photograph includes the following businesses, from left to right: Dennis Crowley's Port Costa Hotel, Jerry Donohue's Bar and Rooming House, Jacob's Store, Raffetto's Bar, Lucy's Nevada Saloon, Dick William's Eagle Bar, Ferry Exchange Hotel, a barbershop, the post office, a Wells Fargo office, Boehm's Busy Bee Restaurant, and Emmons Bar. The photograph at left shows John O'Neil's General Store, which sat west of the Port Costa Hotel. Notice the different spellings, "O'Neill" and "O'Neil," on the upper and lower signs. (Both courtesy of Contra Costa Historical Society.)

Early Port Costa was accessible by train and water only. Two ferries, the Modoc and the Apache, made regular supply stops at the public wharf. In the above photograph, the Apache is docked at Port Costa near one of the great wheat ships—the Eaton Hall from Liverpool, England. The photograph below shows the Modoc moving away from the Port Costa wharf up the strait toward Martinez. In 1886, a wagon road was cut from Port Costa to Martinez at a cost of $668 per mile. (Both courtesy of Contra Costa Historical Society.)

A wagon stops in front of Louis Raffetto's saloon on the old waterfront near the ferry terminal. When the waterfront portion of town was demolished in 1921, Raffetto moved his saloon into G. W. McNear's stone office on Canyon Lake Drive. (Courtesy of Contra Costa Historical Society.)

By the early 1880s, the Ferry Exchange Hotel was already in place next to the ferry terminal and was owned by the capricious Judge Jeremiah Casey. The judge was known to render decisions from the balcony of his hotel and mete out lighter justice on the men who frequented his saloon. Mrs. E. P. Lynch owned the hotel by the time this photograph was taken. (Courtesy of Contra Costa Historical Society.)

These two photographs show some of the wheat ships that made Port Costa famous. The above photograph is of a ship being towed away by a tugboat (out of frame to the left). The c. 1890 photograph below shows a young woman aboard the wheat ship *Neville*. In 1885, sailing ships such as these carried away 213,000 tons of wheat from Port Costa's wharves. (Both courtesy of Contra Costa Historical Society.)

This photograph shows waterfront Port Costa looking west from the train station. Some of the early businesses seen are Judge Casey's Ferry Exchange Hotel, E. P. Lynch's California Hotel, John Lucy's Nevada Saloon, Raffetto's Bar, Jacob's Store, Donohue's Bar and Rooms, and Dennis Crowley's Port Costa Hotel. The waterfront consisted mainly of rooming houses and saloons that

catered to working men and travelers. The waterfront section of town was built on a 900-foot section of wharf between the *Solano's* ferry terminal on the east and McNear's Port Costa docks on the west. (Courtesy of Crockett Historical Museum.)

In the above photograph from around 1915, friends and family gather to watch a train depart for Martinez. In the background, the Ferry Exchange Hotel and Lynch's California Hotel are visible. The photograph below shows the same train pulling away from Port Costa Station as it makes its way west toward Martinez. The train is passing under the pedestrian bridge that went from the top of Railroad Avenue across the tracks to the train station. (Both courtesy of Contra Costa Historical Society.)

Carlton Watkins took this photograph shortly after the *Solano* went into service for the Central Pacific Railroad (later the Southern Pacific Railroad). On Monday, November 14, 1879, the *Solano* made a trial run between Benicia and Port Costa. The Wednesday, November 16, 1879, edition of the *Benicia Chronicle* gave a detailed description of the *Solano*. The article reported the boat's dimensions as 425 feet in total length, 116 feet across the beam, and a weight of 3,512 tons. Two 1,500-horsepower walking-beam engines furnished the mode of power. It also had eight boilers and four smokestacks. (Courtesy of Robinson collection.)

Pictured here is the *Solano*'s first captain, E. Morton, in retirement. Two crews of officers manned the new ferry, and their names were Captains E. Morton and Jas K. Remington, first officers Bartholeme Kencht and William Poole, second officers J. Tarbox and John Smith, chief engineer Lowe Hogeboom, and assistant engineers A. A. Winship and Fred Smith. All told, 47 men were employed to run the boat 24 hours a day, seven days a week. (Courtesy of Thomas Rubarth.)

In 1914, a second ferry, the *Contra Costa*, was built by Southern Pacific Railroad and put into service at a second slip added to the Benicia and Port Costa facility. The *Contra Costa* was roughly the same size as her sister ship, the *Solano*, with the principal difference between the two vessels being that the *Contra Costa* had a steel hull. In this photograph, from around 1918, the *Contra Costa* is arriving at the Benicia ferry terminal. In the background, to the left, the Associated Oil tanks are visible on hills east of Port Costa. (Courtesy of Contra Costa Historical Society.)

In this *c.* 1918 photograph, two passengers are seen on the deck of the *Contra Costa* as they make their journey from Benicia to Port Costa. (Courtesy of Contra Costa Historical Society.)

The *Contra Costa*'s slip was originally placed a few hundred yards east of the *Solano*'s slip. This c. 1915 photograph shows a tangle of tracks jutting out at an angle from the mouth of the new *Contra Costa* slip with the *Solano*'s slip visible in the foreground. The *Contra Costa*'s first slip, ravaged by toredo pile worms and strong currents, tore loose and floated away one day. A powerful railroad executive, H. K. Kruttschnitt, then ordered it rebuilt next to the *Solano*'s slip. (Courtesy of Thomas and Bill Rubarth.)

In this February 26, 1920, photograph, the *Contra Costa* is steaming past its battered ferry slip. In retrospect, it makes sense that the ferry was originally berthed east of the *Solano*. There may have been no room for a second ferry slip next to the *Solano* while the old Post Costa waterfront occupied the shoreline. When the old town was razed in 1921, the *Contra Costa* was relocated next to the *Solano* (see page nine). (Courtesy of Crockett History Museum.)

The ferry *Solano* went into service at Port Costa on December 28, 1879. At 420 feet in length, it was the largest ferry in the world. Its deck could accommodate 18 passenger cars and 2 locomotives or 32 freight cars and 2 locomotives.

In this *c.* 1955 photograph, the shoreline still shows the imprint of the old ferry terminals. Railroad cars sit parked on tracks leading to where the *Solano* once docked. Farther up, the old lighthouse marks the boundary where the *Contra Costa* once came into Port Costa.

Pictured above, more than 70 years since the *Solano*'s removal, the shoreline still bears the contours of the old ferry slip. The below photograph shows one of the cement foundations for the great hinge joints that once allowed the *Solano* to move up and down in the water as the tides changed and the loads on its decks changed during the on- and off-loading procedures. Today the hinge, a curiosity piece, offers a seat for people exploring the shoreline and is a nice pier for local fishermen.

In the above photograph, one of the switch engines, which were derisively referred to as "boat goats," is seen on the deck of the Contra Costa. The boat goats were used to move rail cars on and off the ferries. Below, a railroad switchman tries to hop aboard a passenger car as a boat goat pulls a string of cars from the Contra Costa. (Both courtesy of Contra Costa Historical Society.)

The rush to get trains off and on the boats occasionally led to accidents. In the above image, an engine has run off the end of the pier at the Port Costa slip. One of the ferries is seen in the second slip behind it. Such an occurrence would have greatly impacted the schedule since only one slip would have to service both boats until the obstruction could be cleared. In the below photograph, a smaller boat goat has run, or has been pushed, off the end of the *Solano* at the Benicia terminal. A crane mounted on a flatbed train car had been brought on board to pull the boat goat from the water. (Both courtesy of Contra Costa Historical Society.)

Pictured above are some of the crewmen and railroad men of the *Solano* near the end of its working life. Below, the *Solano* is seen on October 15, 1930, leaving Port Costa for the last time, packed to the gunnels with passengers and festooned with bunting. By 1930, the trains had grown longer, the engines heavier, and the two ferries were insufficient for the workload. A double-track train bridge between Benicia and Martinez replaced the two great boats.

After the ferryboats were retired from service, the younger, steel-hulled Contra Costa was sold to Rosenberg Brothers in 1933, and the hull was cut into three sections and used as barges. The *Solano* enjoyed a more dignified retirement, as it was sold to the Antioch Marina, where it was used as a breakwater and fishing pier. Above, in a c. 1931 photograph, the *Solano* is being scuttled at the Antioch Marina. Below, the *Solano*, stripped to the deck, is seen in the 1970s. On the Fourth of July in 1983, stray fireworks set the old boat ablaze, and it burned to the waterline.

These are the remains of the *Solano* as it appears today. In the center left of the frame is one of the A-frames of the two walking-beam engines that powered the ship. Next to it is a second A-frame that has toppled over. Much of the wreckage has silted in and is overgrown with brush and tress. Many locals refer to the wreckage as "Solano Island." (Courtesy of Thomas Rubarth.)

Pictured here is a working HO scale model constructed by Bill and Tom Rubarth and Jim Turner. The model, which took 15 years to create, was displayed on October 14, 2004, at the Port Costa School. (Photograph by John V. Robinson.)

Two
THE RAILROAD YEARS

After the ferry service ended in 1930, the Port Costa yard remained vital to Southern Pacific Railroad service. The railroad yard remained an important location for local freight service and, since the roundhouse and maintenance facilities were already located at Port Costa, the yard at the foot of Canyon Lake Drive remained in service for 30 more years. Pictured here is the Port Costa Train Station, around 1958, near the end of its active service. The Port Costa yard was closed and the entire operation moved to Martinez in 1960. By 1961, most of the site had been completely removed, and today only a few concrete foundations remain to indicate the scale of the railroad yard in its heyday. (Courtesy of Contra Costa Historical Society.)

For over 50 years, Port Costa was an important crossroads of the transcontinental railroad system. In the above photograph from 1901, a funeral train memorializing the 25th president, William McKinley, passes through Port Costa. Below, Port Costa residents greet the presidential train of William Howard Taft as it rolls off the *Solano* in 1909 during Taft's inaugural tour of the country. (Both courtesy of Contra Costa Historical Society.)

Seen in these two images are some of the equipment and train crews who worked for the Central Pacific, and later Southern Pacific Railroad, in Port Costa for 80 years. Above is a photograph from 1910 of an engine and its crew, and below is an image from the 1940s of a later-model steam engine. In the background, several homes extend up the hill from the top of Railroad Avenue and overlook the Carquinez Strait. These houses burned in the fire of 1983, which ravaged the hills between Port Costa and Crockett. (Both courtesy of Contra Costa Historical Society.)

In this photograph from 1980 is one of the "houses on the hill." Homes like this were built on railroad land and housed railroad workers. When the railroad yard closed and the inhabitants moved or passed away, some of the homes gradually fell into disrepair. This house, like the rest on the hill, was destroyed in the fire of 1983, which also obliterated Eckley and the *Garden City*. (Courtesy of Contra Costa Historical Society.)

The above view from July 1954 shows the roundhouse and turntable as it looked from the western edge of the yard. The turntable was 70 feet long and was operated by the steam generated by the engines themselves. The below photograph, from around 1955, shows two local girls, Sharon Decarlo (left) and Mary-Ann Thomas, near the Southern Pacific roundhouse at the foot of Canyon Lake Drive. (Both courtesy of Mary Ann Robinson.)

These two shots from the mid-1950s show the compactness of the Port Costa yard. Steep bluffs on either side of the mouth of the Bull Valley kept the train yard hemmed in. Still, the yard had everything it needed to service the engines, and it remained in operation until around 1960. (Both courtesy of Contra Costa Historical Society.)

By 1960, the Port Costa yard was in decline, and the decision was made to move its operations five miles west to Martinez. There were, it is believed, two reasons for this: first was the need for more space, and the second was that by 1960 the switch to diesel locomotives was complete and the Port Costa yard, which had been designed to service steam locomotives, was simply outdated. The lower photograph shows the yard being dismantled in 1962. Today the imprint of the old yard is still in place, but the site is used only for parking. (Both courtesy of Contra Costa Historical Society.)

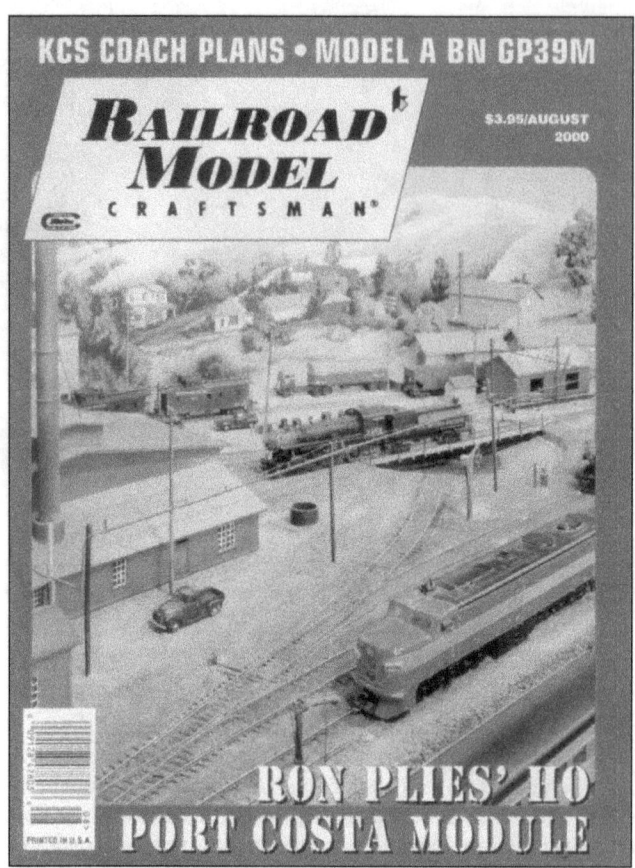

Today the Port Costa railroad yard exists in only HO scale model form. Model railroader Ron Plies constructed a detailed replica of the old Port Costa yard. The model is very accurate in all its details and was featured the August 2000 edition of *Railroad Model Craftsman*. As illustrated earlier in the model of the *Solano*, model railroad buffs have done a wonderful job recreating parts of Port Costa's railroad history. (Both courtesy of Ron Plies.)

Three
BULL VALLEY

This is G. W. McNear who came to Port Costa with the railroad in 1879. He built his Port Costa docks on the waterfront and eventually purchased William Piper's 4,000-acre ranch in Bull Valley south of the Ferry Slip. McNear quickly laid out the town of Port Costa that we know today. (Courtesy of Contra Costa Historical Society.)

The foot of Canyon Lake Drive has changed little in the 40 years between the taking of these photographs. McNear's old warehouse is on the left and McNear's office and the Burlington Hotel are on the right side of the street. Indeed, a photograph from 1890 would look much the same—*sans* the cars that is.

The above view from Railroad Avenue, looking down toward the foot of Canyon Lake Drive, shows the Burlington Restaurant around 1960. At that time, the warehouse was mostly unused, but the lower right corner housed the town fire engine. The photograph below, from around 1977, shows the warehouse when it hosted the popular restaurant Juanita's Galley. The post office has occupied the left corner of the building for at least 60 years. (Both courtesy of Contra Costa Historical Society.)

The above photograph from 1948 shows the Burlington Hotel with a steam engine in the foreground. The Burlington was established in 1883 and, like the warehouse, was originally a two-story structure. A third story was added to both buildings after the 1906 earthquake. It is popularly believed that the Burlington Hotel was once a bordello. Others argue that such an elegant structure on Main Street would never have been used for such nefarious purposes. Below is an image from 1965 that shows the old hotel under renovation.

With its antique furnishings and without telephones or televisions, the Burlington Hotel retains its 19th-century rustic charm. Pictured above is a view of "Kaye's" room. The rooms are not numbered but identified by women's names in keeping with the popular belief that the Burlington was once a bordello. The building has changed little since the 1948 photograph, only the modern vehicles in the picture below indicate that it was taken in the 21st century. (Both courtesy of Veronica Crane and John Robinson.)

This undated photograph at left shows Elizabeth Boehm, whose family managed the Burlington Hotel and operated a restaurant there for many years. Today the space that once housed the restaurant is rented out as an apartment. Below is the inside of the Boehm Restaurant. The Boehm family operated a restaurant in Port Costa for many years and appear in historical records as having a restaurant called the "Busy Bee" on the waterfront near the *Solano*'s ferry terminal as early as 1910. (Both courtesy of Bill and Betty Ligon.)

McNear's famous warehouse was constructed in 1886 and was Contra Costa County's first fireproof building. It was originally two stories tall—a third floor was added after the 1906 earthquake. The outline of the addition is clearly visible in this contemporary photograph. Below is an image from 1968 in which a representative from the phone company (center) presents Bill Rich (left) and honorary mayor and town barber Angelo Coppa with a copy of a local phone book—Port Costa had just gone to the direct-dial system.

This March 1967 edition of *East Bay* magazine announces Port Costa's reemergence as a tourist spot. The post office on the cover is an easily identifiable icon of the town.

Today the post office has a redesigned facade but still maintains its rustic charm.

After the grain years and a long period of dormancy, the warehouse enjoyed a renaissance in the 1960s and 1970s when it hosted a dozen or so antique shops. Pictured above is Wilma Oliver in her shop, Oliver's Oddities, on the first floor of the warehouse. Below is a detail of the curios from one of her cabinets.

Wilma Oliver had a popular shop that sold old toys, postcards, and other antique ephemera, such as this test-your-grip, Shake Hands with Uncle Sam machine, which only cost 5¢ to use.

Constructed in 1897 by G. W. McNear to be the office for his warehouse and water company, this beautiful stone building has held up well for the last 109 years. In the past, the lower floor housed Raffetto's saloon and Angelo Coppa's barbershop. The right side of the building was known to have served as the post office before moving across to the warehouse in the early part of the 20th century. Today the Bull Valley Inn restaurant occupies the ground floor, and two small apartments are on the second floor.

After the waterfront portion of the town was demolished in 1921, Louis Raffetto moved his bar across the tracks to the McNear Building. Raffetto is pictured above with a customer in 1925. Below, Veronica Crane stands in the same spot 80 years later. The current bar is not Raffetto's but one that was brought from the La Grande Hotel in 1966 by John Domagalski when he owned the Bull Valley Inn.

Dan's Place on Canyon Lake Drive was a popular watering hole in the 1950s. Note the two gas pumps in front. A typewritten account at the Contra Costa Historical Society lists this property as the Burke Hotel in 1907. In the early 1960s, Bill Rich remodeled the building, now called the Wheat Dock, into antique shops on the bottom and apartments on the second floor.

Wendy Addison's Theater of Dreams (right), now occupies the retail space at the front of Wheat Dock. Like many residents, Addison volunteers her time and supports the Port Costa Conservation Society. Below, Addison and her fellow "hobo," Robin Wakeley, pose in costume for their performance of "Haywire Mac" McClintock's "Big Rock Candy Mountain" at the 2006 Port Costa Talent Show. McClintock once worked as a switchman in Port Costa and perhaps got his inspiration for such songs as "Hallelujah, I'm a Bum" from his Port Costa experience.

This c. 1950 photograph (above) shows Bea and Vern Runnells in front of the Port Costa Mercantile. John and Jerry Burke appear in the 1890 Polk Business Directory as saloon owners. By 1907, the Mercantile Building was also listed as belonging to Burke family. In the 1970s and 1980s, the Mercantile Building was an antique shop.

These are two views looking north up Canyon Lake Drive. The above image is from 1948 and is of Pat Mahoney walking his dog up the drive with the roundhouse and a Southern Pacific locomotive in the background. The view below from 2006 looks much the same, except the Southern Pacific yard is now a parking lot, and visitors have a better view across the strait to Benicia.

This undated image, probably from the late 1950s, is of the old Forester's Hall on Canyon Lake Drive north of Erskine Street. Gracie Allen, wife and partner of George Burns, used to ride the ferry over from San Francisco to give dance lessons at the hall. Known in later years as "the annex," it was managed by the Boehm family and served as a rooming house for railroad workers. When the railroad yard moved to Martinez in the early 1960s, the annex was demolished.

This house on the corner of Erskine Street and Canyon Lake Drive was built in the mid-1960s and is best remembered as home to Muriel's Doll House Museum. Muriel Whitmore came to Port Costa from Oregon with her doll collection in the 1960s. The Doll House Museum was open Tuesday through Sunday from 10:00 a.m. to 7:00 p.m.; admission for adults was $1 and 25¢ for children. Muriel Whitmore passed away in July 1990 at the age of 84. Today the dolls are gone, and the house is a private residence.

This house on the corner of South and Erskine Streets is thought to be the oldest in town and is thought to be William Piper's original ranch house. Today the building looks much the same as it did 100 years ago.

Established September 15, 1881, this little building was the original Port Costa Post Office. Oral histories report the building first sat on the waterfront portion of town when Kate Hurley was the postmaster. When Hurley retired in 1915, the railroad moved the building next to her house to Second Avenue, where it sits today. By 1915, the post office had outgrown the little building and, after passing through the McNear office building, eventually found a new home on the ground floor of the warehouse.

ORIGINAL PORT COSTA POST OFFICE, EST. SEPT. 15, 1881

These two photographs from 1905 (above) and 2006 (below) show the west side of town, which runs into the steep hills above the Bull Valley. They both give a good indication of where the waterfront community is situated relative to the existing town. In the older image, the warehouse and the Burlington Hotel are two stories tall. After the 1906 earthquake, third stories were added to both buildings, which somewhat obscure the view of the modern photograph. The houses that perch on the hill above the waterfront burned in the fire of 1983.

The Railroad House at No. 2 Railroad Avenue, pictured c. 1900, is the three-story structure above, in the center. Pat Mahoney owned the bar and boardinghouse, and George McNear wanted them. McNear reportedly offered Mahoney three times the building's worth, but the stubborn Irishman refused to sell. In frustration, McNear cut off Mahoney from the town's water supply. Mahoney drilled a well through the floor of his own kitchen and stayed in business long after McNear's 1909 death.

In the late 1940s, Roy Hunter arrived in Port Costa and eventually purchased the old Railroad House and opened a bait shop/liquor store. Roy Hunter is pictured above in front of Hunter's Bait Shop (1965) and below later in life, sitting in front of the Burlington Hotel. Hunter had a habit of calling everyone "cousin" or "cuz," and so the town dubbed him "Cuzzy," a moniker he cheerfully accepted.

The fire department is pictured above doing a controlled burn on one of the last of the railroad depot buildings around 1962. In 1984, the site was declared the Ernie Bernal Memorial Grove, seen below, in memory of Ernie Bernal, a kindly man who lived for many years in an apartment above the Bull Valley Inn.

Maintaining Port Costa's pioneering spirit and community activism, residents created the first curbside recycling program in Contra Costa County. Between 1982 and 1994, the town collected over 500 tons of materials worth $22,500 and used it for a fund to care for Port Costa's trees. Shown above in 1989 are volunteers, from left to right, Ridge, Claire, Monica, and Aaron Green, Jenna Holmes, Andrea Walters (in front), Diane Stewart, Mary List, Mitchell (in front) and Janet Walters, and Frank Jurik. In 1982, locals formed the Port Costa Conservation Society to protect the town's heritage and preserve open space around the town. Through grants, memberships, volunteer labor, and fund-raisers, such as the Port Costa Talent Show, pictured below, the society is working to restore the historic Port Costa School, which is listed on the National Register of Historic Places.

The above 1909 photograph by Benicia's Frank J. Stumm was from a series of penny postcards featuring Port Costa. The image shows the town looking north towards Benicia. The little schoolhouse on the right was replaced by a larger brick structure in 1911. The little building on the far left was the Presbyterian Church. Saint Patrick's Church is seen to the right, and the smokestacks of the Solano are visible in the distance. The modern photograph below shows that the southern half of town has changed little in the past 97 years. The larger school obscures the view a bit. The little house in the lower left of both photographs is still standing but is much worse for wear today, as no one has lived there for many years.

"The Lake," as it is commonly known, was formed by a dam constructed in 1910 by G. W. McNear's Port Costa Water Company. It is fed by a natural spring that percolates from the hills a bit higher up the canyon. Today the site is overgrown with trees and appears to be an actual natural lake.

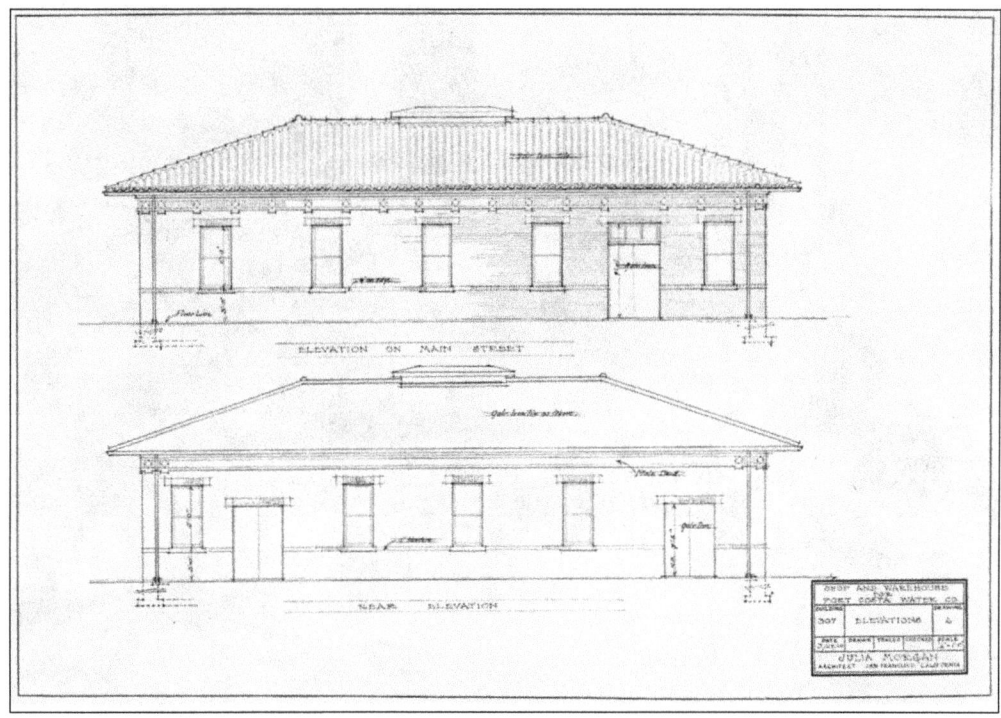

The famous architect Julia Morgan designed the Port Costa Water Company Building. Morgan had worked previously with John Galen Howard, designing some of the best-known buildings on the UC-Berkeley campus. In 1904, she opened her own office in San Francisco and had a prolific career designing hundreds of structures, large and small. In 1919, William Randolph Hearst commissioned Morgan to design the main building and guesthouses for his ranch in San Simeon. The Port Costa Water Company Building was purchased in the mid-1970s and remodeled into a residence.

These two snapshots give a glimpse into early-20th-century Port Costa. The above image shows the McNear water wagon in front of Forester's Hall around 1910. In photograph at left, town children follow an elephant up Canyon Lake Drive toward the ball field where the circus would be setting up its tents.

Built in 1898 on land donated by G. W. McNear, Saint Patrick's Church has served the people of Port Costa for over 100 years. The stained-glass windows bear the names of the people who donated them. Names on the windows, such as J. P. Casey, E. O'Neill, and John Burke, harken back to long-gone waterfront hotels and saloons and the people who owned them. Saint Patrick's is a popular subject for artists who come to paint, sketch, and photograph the historic buildings of Port Costa.

Port Costa has long had a volunteer fire department. The local fire engine has been housed in several buildings throughout the years, including McNear's warehouse in the 1950s. For the past 25 years or so, the Port Costa Fire Department has been in this building on Canyon Lake Drive. Below is a snapshot of the Port Costa Volunteers c. 1996. Pictured from left to right are Doug Stuart, Michael Johnston, Clayton Bailey, Tami Stuart, James Coulter, and Terry Parker. (Below photograph by Doug Stuart.)

The current Port Costa School was built in 1911 and served as the community's grammar school for 55 years until it closed in 1966. The above photograph shows the new school and student body c. 1915. Pictured below is the eighth-grade graduating class of 1953 on the steps of the school. From left to right they are (first row) Mary Ann Thomas, Utanna Smith; (second row) Melvin Freitas, Jim Huey, Jim DeCarlo, teacher Ed Mitchell; (third row) Charles White, Sandy McLendon, Audrey Cooper, Janet Menzies, Judy Voris.

The student body of the Port Costa Grammar School poses on the front steps c. 1946. Pictured here from left to right are (first row) Jerry Falkenstein, Tom Donohue, Sharon Robinson, Walter Vasquez, Carol Amsbury, Ben Palacio, Mary Carr, Rosie Vasquez; (second row) Ed Palacio, Westley Westbrook, Maria Halobious, Don Ligon, Bobby Flockart, Julia Gutierez, Melvin Freitas, Mary Ann Thomas; (third row) Dan Donohue, Sandy McLendon, Don Robinson, Shirly Batchlor, Frank Miller, Francis Guitierez, Bob Parker, unidentified; (fourth row) unidentified, Catherine Huey, Terresa Silva, Mary Stevens, Richard Remkey, Dave Gaffaney, Bob Masek, Bob Norton, James Satori, Mrs. Maloney; (fifth row) Mrs. Lowery, Charles Robinson, Beverly Humphrey, Ruby McDonald, Neva Huey, Marilyn Runnells, Walter Ligon, Howard Helms, Gene Beard; (sixth row) Milo Beard, Dave Stevens, Allan Gaffaney, Bill McLendon, Marcelina Padila, Annie Perez, Donna Stone, Eddy Gaffaney; (seventh row) Jack Jardine, Nelda Kedney, Muriel Fosgate, Rosie Silva, Lauren Norton, unknown, Mary-Ann Mossina, Rachel Perez; (eighth row) Claude Crowe, Richard Kedney, Hugh Whttiker, two unidentified, teacher Bob Jones.

Baseball was a popular pastime in early Port Costa, as it was all across the country in the late 19th century. Nearly every town had a team or two, and Port Costa was no different. In the portrait at right, four young men are seen, c. 1890, posing in their baseball uniforms. The photograph below, from somewhere between 1897 and 1905, is of the Port Costa Flour Mill team, which was owned and operated by G. W. McNear at the time.

The baseball games were played at the field next to the Port Costa Grammar School. The above c. 1915 photograph shows another Port Costa team. Below, yet another team, in black with the YMI (Young Men's Institute) insignia, is taking the field. Note the large grandstand and the newly planted eucalyptus trees on the hillside.

Pictured here are the field and school as they appear today. The school now serves as a town meeting hall and hosts several annual events. This modern photograph shows that the field is still serviceable, though it has been a long time since the town has had a team. The Port Costa Conservation Society has long maintained the school and field.

One of the many volunteers who have kept the school grounds in shape through the years is Frank Jurik, who regrettably passed away in August 2006 at the age of 77. Frank was a founding member of the Port Costa Conservation Society and was known as the unofficial mayor of Port Costa. Frank's presence will be greatly missed.

These two c. 1920 photographs represent some of Port Costa's many residents who worked and lived in town throughout the years. The above image shows a crew for the Valley Tower Lines. Pictured from top to bottom are Mike Necot, tower man; John Kenney, section boss; and Frank Harrington, signal maintenance. The photograph below shows three young women in their Sunday best. Pictured c. 1925 from left to right are Anna Ahern, Nora Ahern, and an unidentified friend. Anna and Nora lived their whole lives at the corner of Reservoir Street and Canyon Lake Drive across from the school.

Pictured above c. 1948 are, from left to right, Rose Smith, Angelo Coppa, the town constable, and Mrs. Raffetto in front of Coppa's Barber Shop in what is now the Bull Valley Inn's dining room. In the early 1960s, Angelo Coppa moved his shop a few doors up Canyon Lake Drive. In the below image, from around 1960, are George McGrath (left) and Angelo Coppa behind Louis Raffetto's old bar, which Coppa kept after Raffetto's death.

Port Costa has always attracted an eclectic mix of people. One of the most colorful was Juanita Musson, who ran the Warehouse Café in the late 1970s. Musson, who weighed 300 pounds, wore colorful muumuus and cussed like a sailor. She was an eccentric character, and her restaurant, Juanita's Galley, attracted a loyal clientele that followed her to several restaurants around northern California from Sausalito to Port Costa to Vallejo and beyond.

Pictured at left in July 1976, Juanita Musson "bones up" on her Kaolithic history as she ponders one of Dr. Gladstone's artifacts from the Wonders of the World Kaolithic Museum on the second floor of the warehouse. (Photograph by Lewis Stewart.)

Artist Clayton Bailey, pictured above c. 1980, taught ceramics for many years in the art department at California State University, Hayward. Below, Bailey is shown with some of the whimsical sculptures he makes out of found objects. Bailey is also known for his Wonders of the World Museum, where his alter ego, Dr. Gladstone, displayed his many discoveries from the Kaolithic and Pre-Credulous eras.

Seen above is Dr. Gladstone at the entrance to the Wonders of the World Museum, where admission was 25¢. Below, honorary mayor Angelo Coppa, in his tuxedo, welcomes Dr. Gladstone and his Kaolithic fossil collection to the second floor of the Port Costa Warehouse. Angelo Coppa cut the ceremonial ribbon, opening the display to the public, and declared the collection to be "very impressive." The specimen pictured here is said to be the greatest Kaolithic giant that "broke the bone barrier." (Both photographs by Lewis Stewart.)

Seen here is the poster announcing the opening of the Wonders of the World Museum on the second floor of the Port Costa Warehouse. Before moving to the warehouse, many of the artifacts and curios were previously exhibited at the De Young Museum of San Francisco in 1975. *Zap Comix* artist S. Clay Wilson illustrated the poster, which advertised, among the day's events, such things as music from Port Costa's The Companion Band, a medicine show featuring Dr. Snootful's Wonder Cure, Dr. Gladstone's attempt to make life out of mud, and a comic book reading by S. Clay Wilson. The Wonders of the World Museum was a popular attraction for the two and a half years it was housed at the warehouse.

Dr. Gladstone discovers a skeleton of Bigfoot in the hills near Port Costa. The story of Dr. Gladstone's finding was featured on the front page of *The Unnatural Enquirer*. (Photograph by Lewis Stewart.)

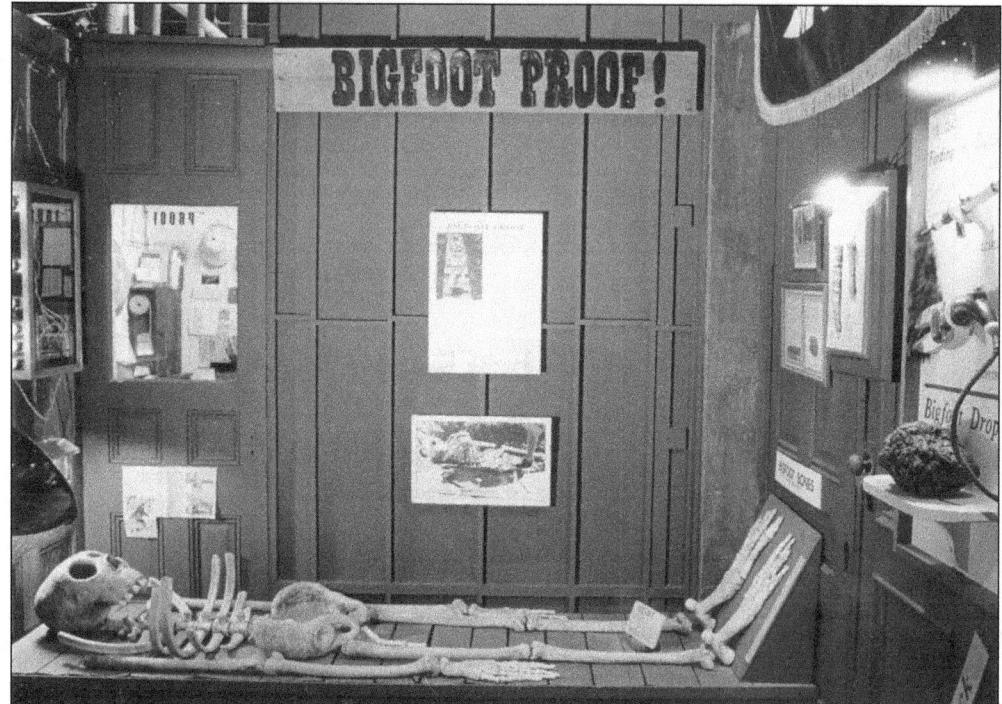

"Bigfoot Proof" was on display at the Wonder's of the World Museum in Port Costa from 1976 through 1978. (Photograph by Lewis Stewart.)

Pictured at right in 1980 is Clayton Bailey with perhaps his most famous creation, *On/Off*, which was built to attract customers to the Wonders of the World Museum. *On/Off*, which could walk and talk, would dispense post cards for 25¢ and was known to use hypnosis to entice customers to the museum. Below, *On/Off* meets Nobel laureate Glenn Seaborg (far left) at the Lawrence Hall of Science at UC-Berkeley. (Above photograph by Betty Bailey; below by Donovan Connaly.)

Bailey is perhaps best known for the small army of robots he has created in his Port Costa workshop. The above image from 2005 shows him in his studio among some of his metal sculptures. The photograph below depicts a few robots in Bailey's studio. Note, the *Bender* robot peering at *Marilyn Monrobot*. (Both photographs by John V. Robinson.)

Four

THE PORT COSTA BRICK WORKS

About a half mile east of Port Costa sits the Little Bull Valley. Today it is known for the brick-making plant that has occupied the valley for 90 years. Known locally simply as "the brickyard," the site was first occupied by the Nevada Warehouse and Dock Company. James Flood and John MacKay, who made their fortunes in Nevada Silver, completed the Nevada Docks in 1883. The dock's 3,000 feet of wharf space was the largest on the strait. Pictured here is the office of the Nevada Docks with its elevated tracks and covered sheds, which made loading faster and easier in all weather. An 1889 county survey shows the site contained several buildings, mostly saloons, and the Shamrock Hotel.

The photograph above, from around 1900, shows the immense size of the Nevada Docks complex. Fires ravaged the docks and warehouses along the waterfront at regular intervals. By the early 1900s, the wheat industry that made Port Costa famous was in decline and shipping interests were moving their operations to San Francisco. The industrial evolution of the site is pretty straightforward. After the Nevada Docks burned in 1909, the Port Costa Brick Works expanded to the waterfront, which made moving bricks by water and rail easier. In the 1920s, Associated Oil arrived in the hills above the brickyard. Associated Oil closed in 1960s. The photograph below shows the site today. It is currently being restored to its natural state.

This reproduction at right of Homestake Mining's company publication *Sharp Bits*, from May of 1965, shows the brickyard as it looked in 1913. Homestake Mining had just purchased the plant from Bob Berg and had devoted an entire issue of *Sharp Bits* to the history of the Port Costa Brick Works. Below is a crew of workmen unloading bricks by hand onto a brick cart. Notice how young some of the workers look. (Both courtesy of Mossina collection.)

These two men were vital in the daily operations of the Brick Works. Pictured above c. 1925 is Bob Berg, the son of founder Chris Berg. In the image below is Lawrence Mossina, a lifelong employee of the Port Costa Brick Works. Mossina eventually worked his way up to vice president. He also took hundreds of photographs documenting every aspect of the plant's development through the years. He took many of the photographs in this chapter. (Both courtesy of Mossina collection.)

In the image at right from 1964, Lawrence Mossina (left) and Bob Berg inspect one of the many innovations they jointly introduced to the plant, a piggyback system that allowed a forklift to be carried on the truck with a load of bricks. Below, in a photograph from 1928, are the office, yard, and some of the company's fleet of trucks. Some of the trucks have hard, solid rubber tires. (Both courtesy of *Sharp Bits*.)

The following two pages show the progression of trucks used to haul bricks from the 1920s through the 1960s. The truck in the above 1920s photograph carried about a ton of bricks. The c. 1930 image below shows a later-model truck and trailer at the Port Costa Yard. (Both courtesy of Mossina collection.)

Pictured above is a General Motors truck from around 1937. It is equipped with a mechanical loading device that was designed and built at the brickyard to facilitate the loading and unloading of bricks. Below, Art Culver (left) and Harold Sliper inspect a modern Peterbilt tractor-trailer purchased when Homestake Mining Company bought the brickyard from Bob Berg in 1964. The plant was renamed Port Costa Clay Products. (Both courtesy of *Sharp Bits*.)

Initially shale was mined by pick and shovel and transported to the site by mule-powered carts. The plant's capacity was 30,000 bricks per nine-hour day. By the 1920s, the plant was becoming mechanized; steam shovels were quarrying the shale and trucks were transporting the rock to the plant. The massive equipment used at the site today would dwarf the old machines. (Above courtesy of Mossina collection; below photograph by John V. Robinson.)

Breakage and chipping was a common problem in the transport and handling of bricks. One solution was to hand-load bricks onto pallets and load the pallets onto trucks and barges with machines. A derrick is seen above loading pallets of bricks onto the Port Costa Brick Works barge near the Associated Oil warehouse. Below a work gang loads bricks onto the barge. (Both courtesy of Mossina collection.)

In the above *c.* 1929 image, another view of the derrick barge unloading bricks at the shoreline is seen. Before the bridges were built, the water barge was vital to quickly moving bricks around the Bay Area. In photograph below, workers clean up bricks after the derrick boom collapsed. In the background is a nice view of the boiler and winches of the stream-donkey engine that powered the derrick. (Both courtesy of Mossina collection.)

Like many old industrial sites, the most recognizable feature of the brickyard was the smokestack. In 1958, a bolt of lightning hit the 200-foot brick smokestack, toppling a third of it to the ground and gouging a split into its base. Bricks rained across a wide area, but no one was seriously hurt in the freak occurrence. (Both courtesy of Mossina collection.)

After the lightning strike severely damaged the old smokestack, a wrecking ball was brought in (above) to bring down the rest of the structure. A steam shovel was used (below) to remove debris from the site. (Both courtesy of Mossina collection.)

Among the machinery at the Brick Works was a narrow-gauge railroad system (above) that could be extended and easily moved to various parts of the quarry. Carts (below) were loaded by steam shovels and trundled back to the plant for processing. By this time, the plant was producing nearly 100,000 bricks a day. Port Costa bricks were considered among the finest in the world. (Both courtesy of Mossina collection.)

The above photograph shows the brickyard around 1930. It is seen below in November of 1964, with the plant halfway through its renovation after its purchase by the Homestake Mining Company. (Both courtesy of Mossina collection.)

In the above photograph from around 1966, the renovations to the plant are in progress. Moving from left to right, the old wooden structures are slowly being replaced by steel-frame buildings. By 1968, the original plant was completely rebuilt and modernized to include a 175-foot, gas-fired, rotary kiln, below, where aggregate pellets were manufactured. (Both courtesy of Mossina collection.)

This photograph from 1968 shows the redesigned Port Costa Products new brick and lightweight aggregate plant. Mounds of aggregate and a telescoping boom for loading aggregate onto railroad cars can be seen at the bottom. (Courtesy of *Sharp Bits*.)

The photograph above shows the newly rebuilt plant looking north from the hillside; Benicia is in the background. The photograph below depicts the greatly reduced plant in the process of being dismantled. The goal is to restore the site to its original condition. The plant's new owners state that when the demolition is complete, it will be as if the Brick Works never existed—and another piece of Port Costa's history passes into oblivion.

Here Joe Noe makes adjustments to the brick-forming machine that forces green clay through a steel die to form a clay column that will be cut into individual bricks. (Courtesy of *Sharp Bits*.)

After passing through the extruding machine, the column of green clay passes through a rotating wire wheel that cuts the column into individual bricks. Pictured here is Pete Jimenez, who monitors the progress of the clay column through the cutting machine. (Courtesy *Sharp Bits*.)

Above, Joe Noe unloads cut bricks off of a conveyor belt onto carts to be removed to a drying room before finally being placed in a kiln to be fired into finished bricks. Right, Junus Jackson checks the green clay as it passes through the aggregate machine. The strands were broken into random sizes and sent through the rotary kiln to be fired into finished pellets. (Both courtesy of *Sharp Bits*.)

In 1956, a new tunnel kiln was constructed. The project, which cost $400,000, included an enclosure for the kiln, a laboratory, and a machine room. Above, the kiln is under construction, and below, a group of people tours a kiln with the finished product in the background. At this time, the plant was capable of producing 120,000 bricks a day. (Both courtesy of Mossina collection.)

Like many of the businesses that made their home on the Carquinez Strait in the early 20th century, the Port Costa Brick Works had its office in San Francisco. After the 1906 earthquake, the demand for brick to build the city was very high. In these photographs from the mid-1920s, the office and showroom, presumably at the corner of Sixth and Berry Streets, can be seen. Notice the strange contour of the building's roof in the image below. Perhaps it was a short-lived architectural fad. (Both courtesy of Mossina collection.)

A tumbler for making "antique" brick is depicted in the c. 1955 image above. The new bricks were run through the tumbler and came out the other end with a worn appearance. After this process, some paint was splashed haphazardly across the worn bricks, seen below, and the product was ready for market. These "antique" bricks were very popular. (Both courtesy of Mossina collection.)

Manufacturing brick always has been a labor-intensive process. Most of the work in the early years was done by hand. In the above photograph, bricks are loaded onto a cart. This cart seems to have a small motor attached to it. In the image below, a worker is seen pulling a cartload of finished bricks. Each brick weighed six pounds, so the carts were very heavy indeed. (Both courtesy of Mossina collection.)

Above, two workers use a hoisting machine to move a bucket of blue shale to be ground into clay for brick making. Below, two workers use a forklift to unload bricks from an outdoor kiln. (Both courtesy of Mossina collection.)

In the image above, two workers use a lifting frame to remove bricks from an outdoor kiln. Below, the bricks are loaded onto a pallet that would be hauled away with a specially designed hydraulic lift. (Both courtesy of Mossina collection.)

Pictured above is a makeshift hoisting machine lifting a pallet load of bricks onto a handcart. Over the years, the Brick Works developed numerous machines and other devices to make handling bricks safer and easier. The photograph below depicts workers unloading bricks at the San Francisco yard with handcarts. Each cart could hold about 100 bricks, or 600 pounds. The manufacturing and handling of bricks always has been backbreaking labor. (Both courtesy of Mossina collection.)

The above shot from around 1955 shows the shoreline of Little Bull Valley and the former site of the old Nevada Docks. At the top of the frame, the Associated Oil docks are winding around the bend into Port Costa, at the center of the frame is one of the Brick Works storage facilities, and at the bottom right are a barge and the docks of White's Fishing Resort. The photograph below is a detail shot of the fishing wharf east of the brickyard. The sign below the railroad-crossing sign reads, "Bank & Wharf Fishing 50 cents per rod. Pay At Office." The lower sign reads, "Anyone using this wharf and crossing do so at their own risk. Do not cross here without permission of the office." (Both courtesy of Mossina collection.)

On the hills between Port Costa and the Brick Works, Associated Oil had a large complex with a large waterfront terminal. The photograph above was taken from the water around 1950 and shows the expanded plant now with a shipping terminal at the base of the hill with a ship at the terminal docks near where the coal bunker once stood. The photograph below is of a 1964 fire at the oil facility. (Both courtesy of Mossina collection.)

Five
ECKLEY

After the 1906 earthquake, bricks for reconstruction were in high demand. In 1907, a brick-making facility called Carquinez Brick and Tile was established at Eckley's Cove. By 1914, the construction boom ended and the company closed. At the height of its commercial life, Eckley had a dozen or so homes, a train depot, and a hotel, which was razed in 1947. Pictured here is the train depot near the brick company around 1910. (Courtesy of Contra Costa Historical Society.)

Pictured here are two views of Granger's warehouse west of Eckley. The above photograph is from around 1900, when the warehouse was at its busiest. The masts from sailing ships can be seen at Granger's and farther down the shore at the California Wharf and Warehouse Company. The image below, c. 1965, shows the old warehouse and wharf greatly diminished. Today nothing but piles remain to mark the old wharf's existence. (Both courtesy of Contra Costa Historical Society.)

In 1870, John Eckley (1827–1898) purchased from William Piper 350 acres of land in a little cove between Port Costa and Crockett (above). Eckley built a home and a pier for his yacht. In 1875, the Grangers Business Association built a wharf and warehouse along a 1,000-foot strip of waterfront just west of Eckley. The little cove purchased by John Eckley has gone through many transformations in the past 136 years. Today it is a part of the East Bay Regional Park District. Below, Kyle (left), Kathy (center), and Ian Robinson pose beside the entrance to Eckley Pier.

In 1907, the Carquinez Brick and Tile Company (above) was established at Eckley and produced brick for the reconstruction of the Bay Area after the devastating 1906 earthquake. Carquinez Brick and Tile supplied four million bricks to rebuild San Francisco's Palace Hotel. They were loaded onto barges owned by the Carquinez Lighterage Company and shipped to points around the bay. Carquinez Brick and Tile closed in 1914, after the post-earthquake building boom ended, and this one old brick structure (below) stands as a silent witness to Eckley's former brick company.

One of G. W. McNear's competitors in the wheat-shipping business was the California Wharf and Warehouse Company, seen above in its prime, around 1895. When the California grain market started to decline in the early 1900s, the warehouse space was put to other uses. The complex burned to the waterline in 1924, and it was not rebuilt. The deteriorating piles in the contemporary photograph below show the ghostly footprint of the busy wharf and warehouse and testify to the tremendous scale of the old complex.

The shoreline between Port Costa and Crockett is peppered with hundreds of rotting piles that give fishermen and other people who walk the shoreline a glimpse of the massive warehouses and docks that once dominated the landscape from Port Costa to Crockett. Below, someone has used a piece of the driftwood that litters the shoreline to declare his or her allegiance to Crockett.

For many years, a loose collection of houses built on wharves and tenant boats of various kinds filled the waterfront between Crockett and Port Costa. The little community was collectively known as "Scow Town." Looking west from Eckley around 1975, two houses are built over the water (the last vestiges of Scow Town?), and farther down the tracks, a section of the old Granger's warehouse can be seen. The April 2006 image below shows the two houses abandoned and derelict. The two old structures were destroyed by fire in July 2006.

Pictured here is the *Garden City* in its heyday. It was built in 1879 and plied the waters from San Francisco to Vallejo Junction for 50 years before being retired from service in 1929. The Carquinez Bridge, along with the Antioch Bridge and Dumbarton Bridge, all built in the mid-1920s, were the beginning of the end for the Bay Area ferry fleet. The ferry sat idle near the C&H Sugar Refinery for several years before Martin Hallissy purchased and moved it to Eckley in 1936.

The Hallissy family lived on the boat for a period of time and built up a popular fishing resort with the *Garden City* as the principal attraction. The boat once housed the largest dance floor in Contra Costa County. Here, in a 1947 photograph, a steam train rolls past the *Garden City* moored at Eckley. (Courtesy of Contra Costa Historical Society.)

These two cards record some of the scant history of the Eckley Resort. The photograph above is a Christmas card from the 1940s, when Martin Hallissy still owned the ferry. The image below is a business card from the mid-1950s, when Walt Wilson and Dave Ansley were operating the resort. The amenities included a boat rental, fishing pier, berthing, a 4,000-square-foot dance hall for rent, as well as place for private parties and meetings aboard the *Garden City*. (Both courtesy of Contra Costa Historical Society.)

Deep water fishing pier . Rental Boats . Outboard Motors . Berthing
Draft Beer . Pizza . 4000 Sq. Ft. Dance Hall For Rent
Private Parties & Meetings by reservation

ECKLEY FISHING RESORT

Look for the Historic "Garden City" Ferry Boat
1½ MILES EAST OF CROCKETT ON PORT COSTA HIGHWAY

WALT WILSON
DAVE ANSLEY

PHONE CROCKETT 221
POST OFFICE BOX 221
CROCKETT, CALIF.

The resort period lasted until 1961, when the *Garden City* was abandoned to the elements and began to deteriorate. By 1983, the once stately ferry, suffering from years of neglect and abuse from squatters, was collapsing into the mud. The end came in 1983 when a fire consumed the

Garden City and the few remaining homes in the little cove called Eckley. (Courtesy of Contra Costa Historical Society.)

In these photographs from 1980, the old ferry is seen with the Carquinez bridges in the background. The *Garden City* presented an imposing site to anyone walking along the shoreline or passing by on the daily trains. Exploring the shoreline between Port Costa and Eckley reveals many surprising details of the busy port's early life. (Both courtesy of Contra Costa Historical Society.)

Today Eckley and the remains of the *Garden City* are part of the Carquinez Regional Shoreline park system. In this view from 2005, the fishing pier juts out into the strait beside the remains of the burned-out *Garden City*. (Photograph by John V. Robinson.)

Pictured here is one of the *Garden City*'s boilers. At low tide, curiosity seekers and beachcombers can get close enough to touch the wreck. Few visitors to the pier appreciate the history of the old ferry or its significance to the history of the Carquinez Strait. (Photograph by John V. Robinson.)

In these two photographs are some of Eckley's inhabitants. The image at left shows Mamie Gonsalves-Perry (left), around 1920, with her cousin near her family's house in Eckley. In the 1980 photograph below, one of Eckley's last residents (name unknown) stands near the deteriorating *Garden City*. (Both courtesy of Contra Costa Historical Society.)

G. W. McNear's Port Costa docks were among the first constructed along the Carquinez Strait. In the c. 1890 photograph above, the docks are being rebuilt after one of the many fires that periodically ravaged them and the warehouses along the shoreline. The Port Costa docks were among the longest to survive, staying in service until 1941, when a fire destroyed the whole complex. Today the shoreline is dotted with hundreds of piles that indicate the vast scale of the Port Costa docks. (Both courtesy of Contra Costa Historical Society.)

The Seamen's Institute was built in 1899 on the hillside between Eckley and Port Costa. The two-story structure was an Episcopal church mission that offered communion, services, ceremonies, and other social activities to the hundreds of sailors who came to Port Costa on ships from around the world. Ruins of the mission's foundation still remain along the edge of the regional park.

BIBLIOGRAPHY

Bowman, Jane. "Port Costa Wide Awake After A Long, Long Nap." *East Bay.* March 1967: vol. 2, no. 3.

Bailey, Clayton. *The Robot Builder's Manual.* Triton Museum of Art, 1981.

Collier, George C. *From Wheat to Antiques: the Story of Port Costa.* Unpublished Manuscript, 1969.

DePaoli, G. Joan and Dr. Gladstone. *Clayton Bailey: Happenings in the Circus of Life*, Davis, CA: John Natsoulas Press, 2000.

Dillon, Richard, H. *Port Costa: Breadbasket of the World.* San Francisco: The Book Club of California, 1984.

Gladstone, Dr. George (Clayton Bailey). "Catalog of Kaolithic Curiosities and Scientific Wonders." *Wonders of the World Museum.* 1975.

"High Quality Brick." *Sharp Bits.* Homestake Mining Company. Fall-Winter 1969, vol. 20, No. 3.

Masten, Shawn. "Port Costa's doll museum founder dies." *Contra Costa Times.* July 16, 1990.

Murdock, Dick. *Port Costa 1879–1942.* Port Costa, CA: Murdock-Endom Publications, 1977.

Rego, Nilda. "Port Costa Brick Works VP dies." *West County Times.* December 13, 1988.

Tatum, Robert D. *Old Times in Contra Costa.* Pittsburg, CA: Highland Publishers, 1993.

"Port Costa Clay Products." *Sharp Bits.* Homestake Mining Company. May 1965, vol. 16, No. 4.

Stewart, Lewis. "Dr. Gladstone Exposes Truth to Disbeliever." *The Unnatural Enquirer.* July 1976.

Visit us at
arcadiapublishing.com